50 The Vegan Gourmet Recipes

By: Kelly Johnson

Table of Contents

- Spicy Chickpea Tacos
- Creamy Cashew Alfredo Pasta
- Jackfruit Pulled Pork Sandwiches
- Cauliflower Buffalo Wings
- Roasted Butternut Squash Soup
- Vegan Mushroom Wellington
- Sweet Potato and Black Bean Burritos
- Thai Peanut Buddha Bowl
- Quinoa-Stuffed Bell Peppers
- Lentil and Spinach Curry
- Vegan Mushroom Stroganoff
- Avocado Toast with Tomato Basil Salsa
- Vegan Tofu Scramble
- Coconut Lentil Stew
- Chickpea and Spinach Stuffed Pita
- Grilled Portobello Mushroom Steaks
- Eggplant Parmesan
- Sweet Potato Falafel
- Vegan Shepherd's Pie
- Spaghetti Squash Primavera
- Vegan Caesar Salad with Crispy Chickpeas
- Sweet and Sour Tofu Stir-Fry
- Carrot Ginger Soup
- Roasted Red Pepper Hummus
- Spicy Tempeh Lettuce Wraps
- Vegan Mac and Cheese
- Zucchini Noodles with Pesto
- Avocado and Mango Sushi Rolls
- Roasted Cauliflower Steaks with Tahini Sauce
- Vegan Chocolate Avocado Mousse
- Vegan Chickpea Salad Sandwich
- Butternut Squash and Kale Risotto
- Vegan Stuffed Mushrooms
- Mango Coconut Chia Pudding
- Vegan Pad Thai

- Maple-Glazed Brussels Sprouts
- Smoky Sweet Potato and Black Bean Chili
- Vegan Sausage and Peppers
- Lemon Garlic Roasted Chickpeas
- Vegan Baked Ziti
- Vegan Ricotta Stuffed Shells
- Cauliflower Rice Stir-Fry
- Vegan Chocolate Chip Cookies
- Sweet Potato and Quinoa Salad
- Vegan Banoffee Pie
- Grilled Vegetable Skewers with Chimichurri Sauce
- Vegan Tempeh Reuben Sandwich
- Peanut Butter Banana Smoothie Bowl
- Vegan Spinach and Artichoke Dip
- Lemon Poppy Seed Muffins

Spicy Chickpea Tacos

Ingredients:

- 1 can (15 oz) chickpeas, drained and rinsed
- 1 tbsp olive oil
- 1 tsp smoked paprika
- 1 tsp chili powder
- ½ tsp cumin
- ¼ tsp cayenne pepper (optional for extra heat)
- Salt and pepper to taste
- 8 small corn tortillas
- 1 avocado, sliced
- ½ red onion, thinly sliced
- Fresh cilantro, chopped
- Lime wedges, for serving

Instructions:

1. In a skillet, heat olive oil over medium heat. Add chickpeas, paprika, chili powder, cumin, cayenne, salt, and pepper. Cook for 5-7 minutes, stirring occasionally, until the chickpeas are crispy and golden.
2. Warm the tortillas in a dry skillet or microwave.
3. Assemble tacos by placing chickpeas on the tortillas, then topping with avocado, red onion, and cilantro.
4. Serve with lime wedges on the side.

Creamy Cashew Alfredo Pasta

Ingredients:

- 12 oz pasta (such as fettuccine or spaghetti)
- 1 cup raw cashews, soaked in water for 4-6 hours or overnight
- 1 cup water
- 2 tbsp nutritional yeast
- 2 tbsp lemon juice
- 2 cloves garlic
- Salt and pepper to taste
- 2 tbsp olive oil
- Fresh parsley, chopped for garnish

Instructions:

1. Cook pasta according to package instructions.
2. Drain the soaked cashews and blend them with water, nutritional yeast, lemon juice, garlic, salt, and pepper until smooth and creamy.
3. In a skillet, heat olive oil over medium heat. Pour in the cashew cream and simmer for 2-3 minutes to heat through.
4. Toss the cooked pasta in the creamy sauce and serve with fresh parsley.

Jackfruit Pulled Pork Sandwiches

Ingredients:

- 2 cans (14 oz each) young green jackfruit in brine, drained and shredded
- 1 tbsp olive oil
- 1 onion, chopped
- 2 cloves garlic, minced
- 1 cup barbecue sauce
- 1 tbsp apple cider vinegar
- 1 tsp smoked paprika
- 1 tsp cumin
- 8 slider buns or sandwich rolls
- Coleslaw (optional, for topping)

Instructions:

1. In a skillet, heat olive oil over medium heat. Add onion and garlic, cooking until softened (about 5 minutes).
2. Stir in the shredded jackfruit, barbecue sauce, apple cider vinegar, paprika, and cumin. Simmer for 15-20 minutes, stirring occasionally, until the jackfruit is tender and has absorbed the sauce.
3. Toast the buns and assemble sandwiches by placing the jackfruit mixture on the bottom bun and topping with coleslaw, if desired.

Cauliflower Buffalo Wings

Ingredients:

- 1 medium cauliflower, cut into florets
- 1 cup all-purpose flour
- 1 tsp garlic powder
- 1 tsp onion powder
- 1 tsp smoked paprika
- ½ tsp cayenne pepper (optional for extra heat)
- ¾ cup water
- Salt and pepper to taste
- ½ cup buffalo sauce
- 2 tbsp olive oil

Instructions:

1. Preheat oven to 400°F (200°C). Line a baking sheet with parchment paper.
2. In a large bowl, whisk together flour, garlic powder, onion powder, paprika, cayenne, salt, and pepper. Add water to form a thick batter.
3. Dip the cauliflower florets into the batter, coating them evenly, then place them on the baking sheet.
4. Bake for 25-30 minutes, flipping halfway through, until the cauliflower is crispy and golden.
5. In a separate bowl, toss the baked cauliflower with buffalo sauce and olive oil. Serve with vegan ranch or blue cheese dressing.

Roasted Butternut Squash Soup

Ingredients:

- 1 medium butternut squash, peeled, seeded, and cubed
- 1 tbsp olive oil
- 1 onion, chopped
- 2 carrots, peeled and chopped
- 3 cloves garlic, minced
- 4 cups vegetable broth
- 1 tsp ground cinnamon
- ½ tsp ground nutmeg
- Salt and pepper to taste
- Fresh thyme, for garnish

Instructions:

1. Preheat oven to 400°F (200°C). Toss the butternut squash cubes with olive oil and salt, and spread them on a baking sheet. Roast for 25-30 minutes, until tender and lightly caramelized.
2. In a large pot, heat olive oil over medium heat. Add onion, carrots, and garlic, cooking until softened (about 5-7 minutes).
3. Add roasted squash, vegetable broth, cinnamon, nutmeg, salt, and pepper. Simmer for 10-15 minutes.
4. Use an immersion blender to puree the soup until smooth. Adjust seasoning to taste and serve with fresh thyme.

Vegan Mushroom Wellington

Ingredients:

- 1 lb mushrooms (cremini, portobello, or a mix), finely chopped
- 1 tbsp olive oil
- 1 onion, chopped
- 2 cloves garlic, minced
- 1 tbsp fresh thyme, chopped
- 1 tbsp soy sauce
- 1 sheet puff pastry (vegan if needed)
- ¼ cup breadcrumbs
- 1 tbsp Dijon mustard
- Salt and pepper to taste

Instructions:

1. Preheat oven to 400°F (200°C). In a skillet, heat olive oil over medium heat. Add mushrooms, onion, garlic, and thyme, cooking until the mushrooms release their moisture and become golden (about 8-10 minutes).
2. Stir in soy sauce, breadcrumbs, salt, and pepper. Remove from heat and let cool.
3. Roll out the puff pastry on a floured surface. Spread Dijon mustard over the center, then top with the mushroom mixture.
4. Fold the pastry over the mushrooms, sealing the edges. Place on a baking sheet and bake for 25-30 minutes, until golden and puffed.
5. Let cool slightly before slicing and serving.

Sweet Potato and Black Bean Burritos

Ingredients:

- 2 medium sweet potatoes, peeled and diced
- 1 tbsp olive oil
- 1 can (15 oz) black beans, drained and rinsed
- 1 tsp cumin
- 1 tsp smoked paprika
- ½ tsp chili powder
- Salt and pepper to taste
- 4 large flour tortillas
- 1 avocado, sliced
- Fresh cilantro, chopped
- Salsa, for serving

Instructions:

1. Preheat oven to 400°F (200°C). Toss sweet potatoes with olive oil, cumin, paprika, chili powder, salt, and pepper. Roast for 20-25 minutes, until tender.
2. In a bowl, mash the black beans with a fork and stir in roasted sweet potatoes.
3. Warm tortillas in a skillet or microwave. Spoon the sweet potato and black bean mixture onto each tortilla, adding avocado, cilantro, and salsa.
4. Roll up the tortillas into burritos and serve.

Thai Peanut Buddha Bowl

Ingredients:

- 1 cup cooked quinoa
- 1 cup shredded cabbage (purple or green)
- 1 carrot, julienned
- 1 cucumber, sliced
- ½ cup edamame (steamed)
- ¼ cup peanut butter
- 2 tbsp soy sauce or tamari
- 1 tbsp lime juice
- 1 tbsp maple syrup
- 1 tsp grated ginger
- 1 tbsp sesame seeds
- Fresh cilantro, chopped

Instructions:

1. In a bowl, arrange cooked quinoa, shredded cabbage, carrot, cucumber, and edamame.
2. In a small bowl, whisk together peanut butter, soy sauce, lime juice, maple syrup, and ginger to create the peanut sauce.
3. Drizzle the peanut sauce over the bowl and top with sesame seeds and fresh cilantro.

Quinoa-Stuffed Bell Peppers

Ingredients:

- 4 bell peppers (red, yellow, or orange), tops cut off and seeds removed
- 1 cup quinoa, rinsed
- 1 can (15 oz) black beans, drained and rinsed
- 1 cup corn kernels (fresh or frozen)
- 1 onion, chopped
- 2 cloves garlic, minced
- 1 tsp cumin
- 1 tsp chili powder
- ½ tsp smoked paprika
- Salt and pepper to taste
- 1 cup diced tomatoes (canned or fresh)
- Fresh cilantro, chopped (for garnish)
- ½ cup vegan cheese (optional)

Instructions:

1. Preheat oven to 375°F (190°C). Bring 2 cups of water to a boil, then add quinoa. Reduce heat, cover, and simmer for 15 minutes, until cooked.
2. In a skillet, sauté onion and garlic in a little oil over medium heat until softened. Add black beans, corn, diced tomatoes, quinoa, cumin, chili powder, paprika, salt, and pepper. Stir well and cook for 5 minutes to combine.
3. Stuff the bell peppers with the quinoa mixture and place them in a baking dish.
4. Cover with foil and bake for 30 minutes. If using vegan cheese, sprinkle it on top and bake for an additional 5 minutes until melted.
5. Garnish with fresh cilantro and serve.

Lentil and Spinach Curry

Ingredients:

- 1 cup dried lentils, rinsed
- 1 onion, chopped
- 2 cloves garlic, minced
- 1-inch piece fresh ginger, grated
- 1 can (14 oz) coconut milk
- 1 can (14 oz) diced tomatoes
- 2 cups vegetable broth
- 4 cups fresh spinach
- 1 tsp ground cumin
- 1 tsp ground coriander
- 1 tsp turmeric
- 1 tsp curry powder
- ½ tsp cayenne pepper (optional for heat)
- Salt and pepper to taste
- Fresh cilantro, for garnish

Instructions:

1. In a large pot, sauté onion, garlic, and ginger in a little oil over medium heat until softened (about 5 minutes).
2. Add cumin, coriander, turmeric, curry powder, cayenne, salt, and pepper. Stir and cook for 1 minute until fragrant.
3. Add lentils, coconut milk, diced tomatoes, and vegetable broth. Bring to a boil, then reduce heat and simmer for 25-30 minutes, until lentils are tender.
4. Stir in spinach and cook for another 2-3 minutes, until wilted.
5. Serve hot, garnished with fresh cilantro.

Vegan Mushroom Stroganoff

Ingredients:

- 12 oz pasta (egg-free, such as fettuccine or penne)
- 2 tbsp olive oil
- 1 onion, chopped
- 3 cups mushrooms (cremini or button), sliced
- 2 cloves garlic, minced
- 1 cup vegetable broth
- 1 cup coconut milk or other plant-based milk
- 1 tbsp Dijon mustard
- 1 tbsp soy sauce or tamari
- Salt and pepper to taste
- Fresh parsley, chopped for garnish

Instructions:

1. Cook the pasta according to the package instructions. Drain and set aside.
2. In a large skillet, heat olive oil over medium heat. Add onion and garlic, cooking until softened (about 5 minutes).
3. Add mushrooms and sauté for 8-10 minutes, until tender and browned.
4. Stir in vegetable broth, coconut milk, Dijon mustard, soy sauce, salt, and pepper. Bring to a simmer and cook for 5-7 minutes, until the sauce thickens.
5. Toss the cooked pasta in the mushroom sauce. Serve garnished with fresh parsley.

Avocado Toast with Tomato Basil Salsa

Ingredients:

- 2 slices whole-grain bread, toasted
- 1 ripe avocado, mashed
- 1 cup cherry tomatoes, quartered
- 2 tbsp fresh basil, chopped
- 1 tbsp olive oil
- 1 tbsp balsamic vinegar
- Salt and pepper to taste
- Red pepper flakes (optional)

Instructions:

1. In a small bowl, mix together cherry tomatoes, basil, olive oil, balsamic vinegar, salt, and pepper.
2. Spread mashed avocado onto the toasted bread.
3. Top with the tomato-basil salsa and sprinkle with red pepper flakes if desired.
4. Serve immediately as a light lunch or snack.

Vegan Tofu Scramble

Ingredients:

- 1 block (14 oz) firm tofu, drained and crumbled
- 1 tbsp olive oil
- 1 onion, chopped
- 1 bell pepper, chopped
- 1 cup spinach, chopped
- 1 tsp turmeric
- 1 tsp garlic powder
- 1 tbsp nutritional yeast (optional)
- Salt and pepper to taste
- Fresh cilantro, for garnish

Instructions:

1. In a skillet, heat olive oil over medium heat. Add onion and bell pepper, cooking until softened (about 5 minutes).
2. Add crumbled tofu to the skillet, along with turmeric, garlic powder, nutritional yeast (if using), salt, and pepper. Cook for 5-7 minutes, stirring occasionally.
3. Stir in spinach and cook until wilted, about 2 minutes.
4. Garnish with fresh cilantro and serve with toast or in a wrap.

Coconut Lentil Stew

Ingredients:

- 1 cup dried lentils, rinsed
- 1 onion, chopped
- 2 cloves garlic, minced
- 1-inch piece fresh ginger, grated
- 1 can (14 oz) coconut milk
- 1 can (14 oz) diced tomatoes
- 2 cups vegetable broth
- 1 tsp ground cumin
- 1 tsp ground turmeric
- 1 tsp ground coriander
- 1 tsp curry powder
- Salt and pepper to taste
- Fresh cilantro, for garnish

Instructions:

1. In a large pot, sauté onion, garlic, and ginger in a little oil over medium heat until softened (about 5 minutes).
2. Add cumin, turmeric, coriander, curry powder, salt, and pepper. Stir and cook for 1 minute until fragrant.
3. Add lentils, coconut milk, diced tomatoes, and vegetable broth. Bring to a boil, then reduce heat and simmer for 30-35 minutes, until lentils are tender.
4. Adjust seasoning with salt and pepper to taste. Serve hot, garnished with fresh cilantro.

Chickpea and Spinach Stuffed Pita

Ingredients:

- 1 can (15 oz) chickpeas, drained and rinsed
- 1 cup fresh spinach, chopped
- 1 tbsp olive oil
- 1 tbsp tahini
- 1 tbsp lemon juice
- 1 tsp ground cumin
- Salt and pepper to taste
- 4 whole-wheat pita pockets

Instructions:

1. In a skillet, heat olive oil over medium heat. Add chickpeas, spinach, cumin, salt, and pepper. Cook for 5-7 minutes, until spinach is wilted and chickpeas are heated through.
2. Remove from heat and stir in tahini and lemon juice.
3. Cut pita pockets in half and stuff with the chickpea-spinach mixture.
4. Serve immediately, with extra lemon wedges if desired.

Grilled Portobello Mushroom Steaks

Ingredients:

- 4 large Portobello mushrooms, cleaned and stems removed
- 2 tbsp olive oil
- 1 tbsp balsamic vinegar
- 1 tbsp soy sauce or tamari
- 2 cloves garlic, minced
- Salt and pepper to taste
- Fresh parsley, chopped for garnish

Instructions:

1. Preheat grill or grill pan over medium-high heat.
2. In a small bowl, whisk together olive oil, balsamic vinegar, soy sauce, garlic, salt, and pepper.
3. Brush the mushroom caps with the marinade and place them on the grill. Cook for 5-7 minutes per side, until tender and charred.
4. Serve the grilled mushrooms as "steaks," garnished with fresh parsley.

Eggplant Parmesan

Ingredients:

- 2 medium eggplants, sliced into ½-inch rounds
- 1 cup breadcrumbs (use gluten-free if needed)
- 1 cup marinara sauce
- 1 cup vegan mozzarella cheese (shredded)
- ¼ cup nutritional yeast (optional)
- 1 tsp dried oregano
- 1 tsp dried basil
- Salt and pepper to taste
- Olive oil for brushing

Instructions:

1. Preheat the oven to 375°F (190°C). Place eggplant slices on a baking sheet lined with parchment paper and brush with olive oil. Season with salt, pepper, oregano, and basil.
2. Bake for 20-25 minutes, flipping halfway through, until golden and tender.
3. In a baking dish, layer marinara sauce, eggplant slices, breadcrumbs, and vegan mozzarella cheese. Repeat layers, finishing with a top layer of cheese.
4. Bake for another 15-20 minutes until the cheese is melted and bubbly.
5. Serve hot, garnished with fresh basil if desired.

Sweet Potato Falafel

Ingredients:

- 2 medium sweet potatoes, peeled and cubed
- 1 can (15 oz) chickpeas, drained and rinsed
- 1 small onion, chopped
- 2 cloves garlic, minced
- 1 tbsp ground cumin
- 1 tbsp ground coriander
- 1 tsp ground turmeric
- 2 tbsp fresh parsley, chopped
- 1 tbsp tahini
- Salt and pepper to taste
- ¼ cup flour (chickpea flour works well)
- Olive oil for frying

Instructions:

1. Boil sweet potatoes in a pot of water for 15-20 minutes until tender. Drain and mash them.
2. In a food processor, combine mashed sweet potatoes, chickpeas, onion, garlic, cumin, coriander, turmeric, parsley, tahini, salt, and pepper. Process until smooth. If the mixture is too wet, add flour to help bind it together.
3. Shape the mixture into small balls or patties.
4. Heat olive oil in a skillet over medium heat and fry falafel for 3-4 minutes on each side, until golden brown.
5. Serve warm with pita bread, tahini sauce, and vegetables.

Vegan Shepherd's Pie

Ingredients:

- 4 large potatoes, peeled and cubed
- 1 cup frozen peas
- 1 cup carrots, diced
- 1 onion, chopped
- 2 cloves garlic, minced
- 1 can (15 oz) lentils, drained and rinsed
- 1 cup vegetable broth
- 2 tbsp tomato paste
- 1 tbsp soy sauce
- 1 tsp dried thyme
- Salt and pepper to taste
- 1 tbsp olive oil

Instructions:

1. Boil potatoes in a large pot for 10-15 minutes until tender. Drain and mash with a bit of olive oil, salt, and pepper.
2. In a large skillet, sauté onion, garlic, carrots, and peas in olive oil over medium heat until soft (about 7 minutes).
3. Add lentils, vegetable broth, tomato paste, soy sauce, thyme, salt, and pepper. Cook for 5 minutes, stirring occasionally, until the mixture thickens.
4. Preheat the oven to 375°F (190°C). Transfer the lentil mixture to a baking dish and top with the mashed potatoes.
5. Bake for 20 minutes, until the top is lightly browned. Serve hot.

Spaghetti Squash Primavera

Ingredients:

- 1 medium spaghetti squash
- 1 tbsp olive oil
- 1 zucchini, sliced
- 1 bell pepper, sliced
- 1 cup cherry tomatoes, halved
- 2 cloves garlic, minced
- 1 tbsp balsamic vinegar
- Fresh basil, chopped for garnish
- Salt and pepper to taste

Instructions:

1. Preheat the oven to 400°F (200°C). Slice the spaghetti squash in half lengthwise and remove the seeds. Drizzle with olive oil, salt, and pepper. Place cut-side down on a baking sheet and roast for 40-45 minutes, until tender.
2. While the squash is baking, heat olive oil in a skillet over medium heat. Sauté zucchini, bell pepper, and cherry tomatoes for 5-7 minutes until soft. Add garlic and cook for an additional minute.
3. Once the squash is done, use a fork to scrape the flesh into spaghetti-like strands.
4. Toss the spaghetti squash with the sautéed vegetables and balsamic vinegar. Garnish with fresh basil before serving.

Vegan Caesar Salad with Crispy Chickpeas

Ingredients:

- 1 large head of romaine lettuce, chopped
- 1 can (15 oz) chickpeas, drained and rinsed
- 2 tbsp olive oil
- 1 tbsp nutritional yeast
- 1 tsp garlic powder
- 1 tsp smoked paprika
- Salt and pepper to taste
- ½ cup vegan Caesar dressing (store-bought or homemade)

Instructions:

1. Preheat the oven to 400°F (200°C). Toss chickpeas with olive oil, nutritional yeast, garlic powder, smoked paprika, salt, and pepper. Spread them out on a baking sheet.
2. Roast chickpeas for 20-25 minutes, shaking the pan halfway through, until crispy.
3. In a large bowl, toss chopped lettuce with vegan Caesar dressing. Top with crispy chickpeas.
4. Serve immediately, garnished with additional nutritional yeast if desired.

Sweet and Sour Tofu Stir-Fry

Ingredients:

- 1 block (14 oz) firm tofu, pressed and cubed
- 1 tbsp cornstarch
- 2 tbsp sesame oil
- 1 bell pepper, sliced
- 1 onion, sliced
- 1 cup pineapple chunks
- 2 cloves garlic, minced
- ¼ cup soy sauce or tamari
- 2 tbsp rice vinegar
- 2 tbsp maple syrup
- 1 tbsp ketchup
- 1 tsp grated ginger
- 1 tbsp sesame seeds (optional)

Instructions:

1. Toss tofu cubes with cornstarch to coat evenly. Heat sesame oil in a skillet over medium-high heat. Fry tofu until golden and crispy, about 8-10 minutes.
2. Remove tofu and set aside. In the same skillet, add bell pepper, onion, and pineapple, cooking for 5-7 minutes until softened.
3. Add garlic, soy sauce, rice vinegar, maple syrup, ketchup, and ginger. Stir well and bring to a simmer.
4. Return tofu to the skillet and toss to coat in the sauce. Cook for an additional 2-3 minutes.
5. Garnish with sesame seeds and serve over rice or noodles.

Carrot Ginger Soup

Ingredients:

- 6 large carrots, peeled and chopped
- 1 onion, chopped
- 2 cloves garlic, minced
- 1-inch piece fresh ginger, grated
- 4 cups vegetable broth
- 1 can (14 oz) coconut milk
- 1 tbsp olive oil
- Salt and pepper to taste

Instructions:

1. In a large pot, heat olive oil over medium heat. Sauté onion, garlic, and ginger until softened (about 5 minutes).
2. Add carrots and vegetable broth, bringing the mixture to a boil. Reduce heat and simmer for 20 minutes, until carrots are tender.
3. Blend the soup using an immersion blender or in batches in a regular blender until smooth.
4. Stir in coconut milk, salt, and pepper. Heat through before serving.

Roasted Red Pepper Hummus

Ingredients:

- 1 can (15 oz) chickpeas, drained and rinsed
- 1 roasted red pepper, peeled and chopped (use jarred or roast your own)
- 2 tbsp tahini
- 1 tbsp olive oil
- 1 tbsp lemon juice
- 1 clove garlic, minced
- ½ tsp cumin
- Salt and pepper to taste
- Fresh parsley, for garnish

Instructions:

1. In a food processor, combine chickpeas, roasted red pepper, tahini, olive oil, lemon juice, garlic, cumin, salt, and pepper.
2. Process until smooth, adding water if needed to reach the desired consistency.
3. Transfer to a bowl and garnish with fresh parsley.
4. Serve with pita, crackers, or veggies.

Spicy Tempeh Lettuce Wraps

Ingredients:

- 1 block tempeh, crumbled
- 1 tbsp olive oil
- 2 cloves garlic, minced
- 1 small onion, diced
- 1 red bell pepper, diced
- 2 tbsp soy sauce or tamari
- 1 tbsp rice vinegar
- 1 tbsp sriracha (adjust to spice preference)
- 1 tsp maple syrup
- 1 tbsp fresh lime juice
- 1 tsp sesame oil
- 1 tbsp fresh cilantro, chopped
- 1 head of butter lettuce, leaves separated
- Salt and pepper to taste

Instructions:

1. Heat olive oil in a skillet over medium heat. Add garlic and onion, sautéing for 2-3 minutes until fragrant.
2. Add crumbled tempeh and cook for 5-7 minutes until golden and slightly crispy.
3. Stir in red bell pepper, soy sauce, rice vinegar, sriracha, maple syrup, and sesame oil. Cook for another 2-3 minutes until the sauce thickens.
4. Season with salt, pepper, and lime juice. Remove from heat and stir in fresh cilantro.
5. Spoon the tempeh mixture into lettuce leaves, serve immediately.

Vegan Mac and Cheese

Ingredients:

- 2 cups elbow macaroni (or any pasta of choice)
- 1 cup cashews (soaked in water for 4 hours or overnight)
- 1 cup water
- 1 tbsp lemon juice
- 2 tbsp nutritional yeast
- 1 tsp garlic powder
- 1 tsp onion powder
- 1 tsp turmeric (for color)
- Salt and pepper to taste
- 2 tbsp olive oil
- Fresh parsley for garnish (optional)

Instructions:

1. Cook the macaroni according to package directions. Drain and set aside.
2. In a blender, combine soaked cashews, water, lemon juice, nutritional yeast, garlic powder, onion powder, turmeric, salt, and pepper. Blend until smooth.
3. In a large pan, heat olive oil over medium heat. Pour in the cashew sauce and cook for 2-3 minutes, stirring frequently.
4. Add the cooked macaroni to the sauce and stir until fully coated.
5. Serve with fresh parsley on top, if desired.

Zucchini Noodles with Pesto

Ingredients:

- 4 medium zucchinis, spiralized into noodles
- 1 cup fresh basil leaves
- 2 cloves garlic
- ¼ cup pine nuts (or walnuts)
- ¼ cup nutritional yeast
- ¼ cup olive oil
- Juice of 1 lemon
- Salt and pepper to taste

Instructions:

1. For the pesto, blend basil, garlic, pine nuts, nutritional yeast, olive oil, lemon juice, salt, and pepper in a food processor until smooth.
2. In a large skillet, heat a little olive oil over medium heat. Add zucchini noodles and sauté for 2-3 minutes until tender.
3. Toss the cooked zucchini noodles with the pesto and serve immediately.

Avocado and Mango Sushi Rolls

Ingredients:

- 1 cup sushi rice
- 1 ¼ cups water
- 2 tbsp rice vinegar
- 1 tbsp sugar
- 1 tsp salt
- 1 ripe avocado, sliced
- 1 ripe mango, peeled and sliced into thin strips
- 4 sheets nori (seaweed)
- Soy sauce, for dipping

Instructions:

1. Cook the sushi rice according to package directions. Once done, mix rice vinegar, sugar, and salt, and stir into the rice. Let it cool.
2. Place a sheet of nori on a bamboo sushi mat. Spread a thin layer of rice over the nori, leaving a small border at the top.
3. Place slices of avocado and mango along the center of the rice.
4. Roll the sushi tightly, using the bamboo mat to help shape it. Seal the edge with a little water.
5. Slice into rolls and serve with soy sauce.

Roasted Cauliflower Steaks with Tahini Sauce

Ingredients:

- 1 large head of cauliflower
- 2 tbsp olive oil
- 1 tsp garlic powder
- 1 tsp smoked paprika
- Salt and pepper to taste
- ¼ cup tahini
- 1 tbsp lemon juice
- 1 tbsp maple syrup
- 1-2 tbsp warm water
- Fresh parsley for garnish

Instructions:

1. Preheat the oven to 400°F (200°C). Slice the cauliflower into ¾-inch thick steaks.
2. Drizzle olive oil over the cauliflower steaks and sprinkle with garlic powder, smoked paprika, salt, and pepper.
3. Roast in the oven for 25-30 minutes, flipping halfway through, until golden and tender.
4. For the tahini sauce, whisk tahini, lemon juice, maple syrup, and warm water until smooth.
5. Drizzle tahini sauce over the roasted cauliflower steaks and garnish with fresh parsley.

Vegan Chocolate Avocado Mousse

Ingredients:

- 2 ripe avocados, peeled and pitted
- ½ cup unsweetened cocoa powder
- ¼ cup maple syrup
- 1 tsp vanilla extract
- Pinch of salt
- ¼ cup coconut milk (or almond milk)

Instructions:

1. Blend the avocados, cocoa powder, maple syrup, vanilla extract, salt, and coconut milk in a food processor until smooth and creamy.
2. Adjust sweetness to taste by adding more maple syrup if necessary.
3. Chill the mousse in the refrigerator for at least 30 minutes before serving.

Vegan Chickpea Salad Sandwich

Ingredients:

- 1 can (15 oz) chickpeas, drained and mashed
- 2 tbsp vegan mayonnaise
- 1 tbsp Dijon mustard
- 1 celery stalk, chopped
- 1 small carrot, grated
- 1 tbsp fresh dill, chopped (optional)
- Salt and pepper to taste
- 4 slices bread (gluten-free if desired)

Instructions:

1. In a bowl, mash the chickpeas with a fork until roughly mashed.
2. Stir in the vegan mayo, mustard, celery, carrot, dill, salt, and pepper.
3. Spread the chickpea mixture on a slice of bread and top with another slice. Serve immediately.

Butternut Squash and Kale Risotto

Ingredients:

- 1 medium butternut squash, peeled, seeded, and diced
- 1 tbsp olive oil
- 1 small onion, chopped
- 1 ½ cups Arborio rice
- 4 cups vegetable broth, warm
- 1 cup kale, chopped
- ½ cup nutritional yeast (optional)
- Salt and pepper to taste

Instructions:

1. Preheat the oven to 400°F (200°C). Toss butternut squash cubes in olive oil, salt, and pepper, then roast for 25-30 minutes, until tender.
2. In a large skillet, sauté onion in olive oil over medium heat for 3-4 minutes. Add Arborio rice and cook for 2-3 minutes until the rice is lightly toasted.
3. Gradually add warm vegetable broth, one ladle at a time, stirring constantly and allowing the liquid to absorb before adding more.
4. Once the rice is tender and creamy (about 18-20 minutes), stir in the roasted butternut squash, kale, and nutritional yeast. Serve immediately.

Vegan Stuffed Mushrooms

Ingredients:

- 12 large mushroom caps, stems removed
- 1 cup cooked quinoa
- 1 small onion, chopped
- 2 cloves garlic, minced
- ¼ cup breadcrumbs
- ¼ cup nutritional yeast
- 2 tbsp fresh parsley, chopped
- 2 tbsp olive oil
- Salt and pepper to taste

Instructions:

1. Preheat the oven to 375°F (190°C). Place mushroom caps on a baking sheet.
2. In a skillet, sauté onion and garlic in olive oil over medium heat for 3-4 minutes.
3. Add cooked quinoa, breadcrumbs, nutritional yeast, parsley, salt, and pepper. Stir to combine and cook for 2-3 minutes.
4. Stuff the mushroom caps with the quinoa mixture and drizzle with a little olive oil.
5. Bake for 20-25 minutes until the mushrooms are tender and the filling is golden.

Mango Coconut Chia Pudding

Ingredients:

- 1 cup canned coconut milk (full-fat)
- 1 cup almond milk (or any plant-based milk)
- 2 tbsp maple syrup (or sweetener of choice)
- 1 cup chia seeds
- 1 ripe mango, peeled and diced
- 1 tsp vanilla extract
- Fresh mint leaves for garnish (optional)

Instructions:

1. In a bowl, whisk together coconut milk, almond milk, maple syrup, and vanilla extract.
2. Stir in chia seeds, making sure they are well incorporated.
3. Cover and refrigerate for at least 4 hours or overnight, allowing the chia seeds to absorb the liquid and thicken.
4. Before serving, stir the pudding and top with fresh mango and mint leaves.
5. Serve chilled.

Vegan Pad Thai

Ingredients:

- 8 oz rice noodles
- 1 tbsp sesame oil
- 1 cup tofu, cubed
- 2 cloves garlic, minced
- 1 carrot, julienned
- 1 red bell pepper, sliced
- 1 cup bean sprouts
- 2 green onions, sliced
- ¼ cup tamari or soy sauce
- 2 tbsp peanut butter
- 1 tbsp lime juice
- 1 tsp maple syrup
- Crushed peanuts for garnish
- Lime wedges for serving
- Fresh cilantro for garnish

Instructions:

1. Cook the rice noodles according to package instructions. Drain and set aside.
2. Heat sesame oil in a large skillet or wok over medium heat. Add cubed tofu and cook until crispy, about 5-7 minutes. Remove tofu from the skillet and set aside.
3. In the same skillet, sauté garlic, carrot, and bell pepper for 2-3 minutes until tender.
4. Add the cooked noodles, tamari, peanut butter, lime juice, and maple syrup. Toss to coat the noodles evenly.
5. Stir in the tofu, bean sprouts, and green onions, and cook for another minute.
6. Serve the Pad Thai topped with crushed peanuts, cilantro, and lime wedges.

Maple-Glazed Brussels Sprouts

Ingredients:

- 1 lb Brussels sprouts, trimmed and halved
- 2 tbsp olive oil
- Salt and pepper to taste
- 2 tbsp maple syrup
- 1 tbsp balsamic vinegar
- 1 tsp Dijon mustard

Instructions:

1. Preheat the oven to 400°F (200°C).
2. Toss the halved Brussels sprouts with olive oil, salt, and pepper, and spread them evenly on a baking sheet.
3. Roast in the oven for 20-25 minutes, shaking the pan halfway through, until crispy and golden.
4. In a small bowl, whisk together maple syrup, balsamic vinegar, and Dijon mustard.
5. Drizzle the glaze over the roasted Brussels sprouts and toss to coat. Serve warm.

Smoky Sweet Potato and Black Bean Chili

Ingredients:

- 2 medium sweet potatoes, peeled and diced
- 1 tbsp olive oil
- 1 small onion, chopped
- 2 cloves garlic, minced
- 1 can (15 oz) black beans, drained and rinsed
- 1 can (14 oz) diced tomatoes
- 2 tbsp chili powder
- 1 tsp smoked paprika
- 1 tsp cumin
- ½ tsp cayenne pepper (optional)
- Salt and pepper to taste
- 2 cups vegetable broth
- Fresh cilantro for garnish

Instructions:

1. Heat olive oil in a large pot over medium heat. Add onions and garlic, sautéing for 3-4 minutes until soft.
2. Add the diced sweet potatoes, chili powder, smoked paprika, cumin, and cayenne pepper. Stir to coat the sweet potatoes in the spices.
3. Add black beans, diced tomatoes, vegetable broth, salt, and pepper. Bring to a boil, then reduce heat and simmer for 25-30 minutes until the sweet potatoes are tender.
4. Adjust seasoning with additional salt and pepper, if needed.
5. Serve with fresh cilantro on top.

Vegan Sausage and Peppers

Ingredients:

- 4 vegan sausages (store-bought or homemade)
- 1 tbsp olive oil
- 1 onion, sliced
- 2 bell peppers, sliced (use a mix of colors)
- 2 cloves garlic, minced
- 1 can (14 oz) diced tomatoes
- 1 tsp dried oregano
- Salt and pepper to taste
- Fresh parsley for garnish

Instructions:

1. In a large skillet, heat olive oil over medium heat. Add the vegan sausages and cook according to package instructions, until browned and cooked through. Remove from the skillet and set aside.
2. In the same skillet, add onion, bell peppers, and garlic. Sauté for 5-7 minutes until tender.
3. Add the diced tomatoes, oregano, salt, and pepper. Stir and simmer for 10 minutes, until the sauce thickens.
4. Slice the cooked vegan sausages and add them back to the skillet, stirring to coat them in the sauce.
5. Serve the sausages and peppers with fresh parsley on top.

Lemon Garlic Roasted Chickpeas

Ingredients:

- 1 can (15 oz) chickpeas, drained and rinsed
- 2 tbsp olive oil
- 1 tbsp lemon juice
- 2 cloves garlic, minced
- 1 tsp smoked paprika
- Salt and pepper to taste

Instructions:

1. Preheat the oven to 400°F (200°C). Line a baking sheet with parchment paper.
2. Pat the chickpeas dry with a paper towel to remove excess moisture.
3. Toss chickpeas in olive oil, lemon juice, garlic, smoked paprika, salt, and pepper.
4. Spread the chickpeas in a single layer on the baking sheet.
5. Roast for 25-30 minutes, shaking the pan halfway through, until crispy and golden. Serve as a snack or topping.

Vegan Baked Ziti

Ingredients:

- 12 oz ziti pasta (or penne)
- 1 jar (24 oz) marinara sauce
- 1 cup vegan ricotta cheese
- 1 cup vegan mozzarella cheese, shredded
- ¼ cup fresh basil, chopped
- 1 tbsp olive oil
- Salt and pepper to taste

Instructions:

1. Preheat the oven to 375°F (190°C).
2. Cook the ziti pasta according to package directions, drain, and set aside.
3. In a large mixing bowl, combine the cooked pasta, marinara sauce, vegan ricotta cheese, and half of the vegan mozzarella cheese. Season with salt and pepper.
4. Transfer the mixture to a baking dish and top with the remaining vegan mozzarella cheese.
5. Drizzle olive oil on top and bake for 20-25 minutes until the cheese is melted and bubbly.
6. Garnish with fresh basil and serve.

Vegan Ricotta Stuffed Shells

Ingredients:

- 12 large pasta shells
- 1 ½ cups vegan ricotta cheese
- 1 cup spinach, chopped
- 1 tbsp nutritional yeast
- 1 jar (24 oz) marinara sauce
- 1 tsp dried oregano
- Salt and pepper to taste

Instructions:

1. Preheat the oven to 375°F (190°C).
2. Cook the pasta shells according to package directions, drain, and set aside.
3. In a mixing bowl, combine vegan ricotta cheese, chopped spinach, nutritional yeast, salt, and pepper.
4. Stuff each pasta shell with the ricotta mixture and place them in a baking dish.
5. Pour marinara sauce over the stuffed shells and sprinkle with dried oregano.
6. Cover with foil and bake for 25-30 minutes. Remove foil and bake for an additional 5-10 minutes until bubbly.
7. Serve warm.

Cauliflower Rice Stir-Fry

Ingredients:

- 1 medium cauliflower, grated or processed into rice-sized pieces
- 1 tbsp sesame oil (or any preferred oil)
- 1 onion, diced
- 2 cloves garlic, minced
- 1 cup mixed vegetables (carrots, peas, bell peppers)
- 2 green onions, sliced
- 2 tbsp soy sauce or tamari
- 1 tbsp rice vinegar
- 1 tbsp toasted sesame seeds (optional)
- Salt and pepper to taste

Instructions:

1. Heat sesame oil in a large skillet or wok over medium heat. Add diced onion and garlic and sauté for 2-3 minutes until softened.
2. Add the mixed vegetables and sauté for another 4-5 minutes, until tender.
3. Stir in the cauliflower rice and cook for 5-7 minutes, stirring occasionally, until the cauliflower is tender but not mushy.
4. Add soy sauce, rice vinegar, and green onions. Stir to combine and cook for another 1-2 minutes.
5. Season with salt and pepper to taste, and sprinkle with sesame seeds if desired. Serve warm.

Vegan Chocolate Chip Cookies

Ingredients:

- 1 ½ cups all-purpose flour
- 1 tsp baking soda
- ¼ tsp salt
- ½ cup coconut oil or vegan butter, melted
- ½ cup coconut sugar or brown sugar
- ¼ cup maple syrup
- 2 tbsp almond milk (or any plant-based milk)
- 1 tsp vanilla extract
- ½ cup dairy-free chocolate chips

Instructions:

1. Preheat the oven to 350°F (175°C) and line a baking sheet with parchment paper.
2. In a bowl, whisk together the flour, baking soda, and salt.
3. In another bowl, combine the melted coconut oil, sugar, maple syrup, almond milk, and vanilla extract. Mix well.
4. Gradually add the dry ingredients to the wet ingredients and stir until well combined.
5. Fold in the chocolate chips.
6. Scoop tablespoon-sized portions of dough and place them on the prepared baking sheet. Flatten slightly with your fingers.
7. Bake for 10-12 minutes, until the edges are golden. Let cool on the baking sheet for 5 minutes before transferring to a wire rack to cool completely.

Sweet Potato and Quinoa Salad

Ingredients:

- 2 medium sweet potatoes, peeled and diced
- 1 cup quinoa, rinsed
- 2 cups water or vegetable broth
- 1 cup kale or spinach, chopped
- 1 avocado, diced
- 1/4 cup pumpkin seeds or sunflower seeds
- 2 tbsp olive oil
- 1 tbsp balsamic vinegar
- 1 tsp maple syrup
- Salt and pepper to taste

Instructions:

1. Preheat the oven to 400°F (200°C). Toss diced sweet potatoes with 1 tbsp olive oil and salt, then spread them in a single layer on a baking sheet. Roast for 25-30 minutes, turning halfway through, until tender and golden.
2. While the sweet potatoes are roasting, cook the quinoa. Combine quinoa and water or vegetable broth in a pot. Bring to a boil, then reduce the heat, cover, and simmer for 15-20 minutes, or until the quinoa is fluffy and water is absorbed.
3. In a large bowl, combine the cooked quinoa, roasted sweet potatoes, chopped kale or spinach, avocado, and seeds.
4. In a small bowl, whisk together the remaining olive oil, balsamic vinegar, maple syrup, salt, and pepper. Pour the dressing over the salad and toss gently to combine. Serve immediately or chilled.

Vegan Banoffee Pie

Ingredients:

- 1 ½ cups graham cracker crumbs (or digestive biscuit crumbs)
- ¼ cup melted coconut oil
- 2 bananas, sliced
- 1 can (400g) coconut milk (use only the thick cream portion, chilled)
- ¼ cup coconut sugar
- 1 tsp vanilla extract
- 2 tbsp cornstarch
- ½ cup dairy-free whipped cream (optional, for topping)

Instructions:

1. In a bowl, combine the graham cracker crumbs and melted coconut oil. Press the mixture into the bottom of a pie dish to form a crust. Chill in the refrigerator for at least 30 minutes.
2. In a saucepan, combine coconut milk, coconut sugar, and vanilla extract. Bring to a simmer over medium heat.
3. In a small bowl, dissolve cornstarch in a little water to form a slurry. Stir this into the coconut milk mixture and cook, whisking constantly, until it thickens into a pudding-like consistency (about 5-7 minutes).
4. Remove from heat and let it cool slightly. Pour the coconut mixture over the chilled crust.
5. Layer sliced bananas on top of the coconut filling and refrigerate the pie for 2-3 hours to set.
6. Once set, top with dairy-free whipped cream if desired, and serve chilled.

Grilled Vegetable Skewers with Chimichurri Sauce

Ingredients:

- 1 zucchini, sliced into rounds
- 1 red bell pepper, cut into chunks
- 1 red onion, cut into chunks
- 1 cup cherry tomatoes
- 1 cup mushrooms, whole or halved
- 2 tbsp olive oil
- Salt and pepper to taste

For the Chimichurri Sauce:

- 1 cup fresh parsley
- 2 tbsp fresh oregano
- 2 cloves garlic
- 1 tbsp red wine vinegar
- ½ cup olive oil
- 1 tsp red pepper flakes
- Salt and pepper to taste

Instructions:

1. Preheat the grill to medium-high heat. Thread the zucchini, bell pepper, onion, tomatoes, and mushrooms onto skewers. Drizzle with olive oil and season with salt and pepper.
2. Grill the vegetable skewers for 6-8 minutes, turning occasionally, until they are tender and lightly charred.
3. While the vegetables are grilling, prepare the chimichurri sauce. In a food processor, combine parsley, oregano, garlic, vinegar, olive oil, red pepper flakes, salt, and pepper. Pulse until smooth.
4. Once the vegetables are grilled, remove them from the skewers and serve with chimichurri sauce drizzled on top.

Vegan Tempeh Reuben Sandwich

Ingredients:

- 1 package tempeh, sliced thinly
- 2 tbsp olive oil
- 2 tbsp soy sauce or tamari
- 1 tbsp maple syrup
- 1 tsp smoked paprika
- 8 slices rye bread
- 1 cup sauerkraut, drained
- ½ cup vegan Russian dressing or Thousand Island dressing
- ½ cup vegan Swiss cheese (optional, for melting)
- Vegan butter for toasting bread

Instructions:

1. In a pan, heat the olive oil over medium heat. Add the sliced tempeh and sauté until golden and crispy, about 5-7 minutes.
2. In a small bowl, combine soy sauce, maple syrup, and smoked paprika. Pour the mixture over the tempeh and toss to coat. Continue to cook for another 2 minutes, then remove from heat.
3. Heat a grill pan or skillet over medium heat. Butter one side of each slice of rye bread. Place the bread, butter-side-down, on the pan.
4. Spread a layer of Russian dressing on the unbuttered side of each slice. Layer the tempeh, sauerkraut, and vegan cheese on four slices of bread.
5. Top with the remaining slices of bread, buttered side up. Grill each sandwich for 3-4 minutes on each side, until golden brown and crispy, and the cheese is melted. Serve warm.

Peanut Butter Banana Smoothie Bowl

Ingredients:

- 1 frozen banana
- ½ cup peanut butter (or almond butter)
- ½ cup plant-based milk (almond, oat, or soy)
- 1 tbsp chia seeds
- 1 tbsp maple syrup (optional)
- Toppings: sliced banana, granola, shredded coconut, cacao nibs, or chopped nuts

Instructions:

1. In a blender, combine the frozen banana, peanut butter, plant-based milk, chia seeds, and maple syrup (if using). Blend until smooth and creamy.
2. Pour the smoothie mixture into a bowl and top with your choice of toppings, such as sliced banana, granola, shredded coconut, cacao nibs, or chopped nuts.
3. Serve immediately as a satisfying breakfast or snack.

Vegan Spinach and Artichoke Dip

Ingredients:

- 1 cup canned artichoke hearts, drained and chopped
- 2 cups fresh spinach, chopped
- 1 cup raw cashews, soaked for 4 hours or overnight
- ½ cup nutritional yeast
- 1/3 cup lemon juice
- 1/3 cup water
- 2 cloves garlic
- 1 tsp onion powder
- Salt and pepper to taste
- Olive oil for sautéing

Instructions:

1. In a skillet, heat a small amount of olive oil over medium heat. Add the chopped spinach and sauté until wilted, about 3-4 minutes. Set aside.
2. Drain the soaked cashews and place them in a high-speed blender or food processor. Add the nutritional yeast, lemon juice, water, garlic, onion powder, salt, and pepper. Blend until smooth and creamy.
3. Stir in the sautéed spinach and chopped artichokes. Transfer the mixture to a baking dish.
4. Bake at 375°F (190°C) for 20-25 minutes, until the dip is heated through and golden on top. Serve warm with crackers, bread, or vegetable sticks.

Lemon Poppy Seed Muffins

Ingredients:

- 1 ½ cups all-purpose flour
- ¾ cup sugar (or coconut sugar)
- 1 tsp baking powder
- ½ tsp baking soda
- ¼ tsp salt
- ¼ cup coconut oil, melted (or any preferred oil)
- ¾ cup plant-based milk (almond, soy, or oat)
- 2 tbsp lemon juice
- Zest of 1 lemon
- 2 tbsp poppy seeds
- 1 tsp vanilla extract

Instructions:

1. Preheat the oven to 350°F (175°C). Line a muffin tin with paper liners or grease it lightly.
2. In a large bowl, whisk together the flour, sugar, baking powder, baking soda, and salt.
3. In a separate bowl, mix together the melted coconut oil, plant-based milk, lemon juice, lemon zest, poppy seeds, and vanilla extract.
4. Pour the wet ingredients into the dry ingredients and stir until just combined. Do not overmix.
5. Divide the batter evenly among the muffin cups, filling each about 2/3 full.
6. Bake for 18-20 minutes, or until a toothpick inserted into the center comes out clean. Let cool for a few minutes before transferring to a wire rack to cool completely.

www.ingramcontent.com/pod-product-compliance
Lightning Source LLC
LaVergne TN
LVHW061956070526
838199LV00060B/4159